Get Out Of the Fish!
"The GOOF Principle"
Discovering the Jonah in All of Us.

by

Jay Harvey

Published by Intermedia Publishing Group

ISBN: 978-0-9820458-3-1

Printed in the United States of America by Epic Print Solutions

Table of Contents

Dedication

I dedicate this work to my loving family...

To my wife Shelley, for allowing me to come home and share my visions and dreams even though they scare you to death!

To my 3 wonderful children Dallas, Delaney, and Danner I think about you all the time and I will always love you just as you are.

To my Mom and Dad whom I love more and more each day.

Also, to my good friend A. Browning for taking my phone calls...All the time!

Finally, to my brother in Christ, Dane Hudson. Thank you and always remember...

'Not by might nor by power, but by my Spirit', says the Lord Almighty.

Zecharia 4:6 (NIV)

Foreword by Robin Wood

Every now and then, not very often mind you, someone has a real fresh new word from God. I am an avid reader and have read hundreds of new books. I usually read 4 to 5 new books a month. However, there aren't many books that grab my attention. In fact, I rarely recommend books and have only recommended two this year. That included my own new book. Hope you are smiling.

So when asked to read, "Get Out Of the Fish," I thought I'd skim it quickly and put it aside. Nice regular normal read, Wow Was I ever wrong? The word GOOF had my attention big time for two reasons. First, I am a big goof. Over the past 5 years, I have had to "Get Over Myself" "Own My Stuff" "Open Up to God" and hardest of all…I had to "Forgive Myself". Wish Jay had written his book 5 years ago. Maybe a friend would have given me this great read after my personal crash and divorce. I thought I'd go for a big GOOF!

I believe this book has the potential to turn your life around Jay's story of recovery helped this Adrenaline Addict in so many ways. God has provided a personal fish so many times to help me stop and get the sea-weed untangled from around my head.

The rest of my life, I am going to use this fresh concept "GOOF" from Jay Harvey to stay in recovery.

Words cannot express my thanks to you Jay for making me laugh at myself and seek God at the same time. I know I will be giving your book to at least 50 people. So if you are stuck in your own stuff and God has been good to you and provided a fish, then GOOF your way back to wholeness. "Get Over Yourself…Own Your Stuff…Open Up To God…Forgive Yourself…and Forge On!" This book is for you and every important person in your world that you truly care about.

Let's GOOF our way back to God.

Introduction

I know, I know, the last thing we need in this world is another principle to live by. We are swamped with self-help techniques and methods to help us move forward in a more productive, self-affirming way. There are thousands of techniques, motivational tapes, life coaches, ying and yang, karma, etc....etc....You get my drift.

You're probably saying.... "Isn't that what you're doing?" The answer is no.

I did not set out to dream up this principle but I do believe it has merit. This is not self-help, a motivational technique or a secret by any stretch of the imagination. This is something I believe people need; A healthy dose of the truth. I set out to write the book in an effort to help people understand the nature of God and His loving character from what I learned about myself in reading the story of Jonah. I found my life story in the book of Jonah and it all started with one word: *Provision.* Once I realized that Jonah was inside a fish because that is what God had provided as a way to save him.....it all started to make sense for me.

There are common traits we all share with Jonah throughout his story in the Bible. He ran, we run. He denied, we deny. He was down but got back up. He had to open up to God and learn how to forgive others; we can choose to do the same.

So, what emerged for me was a something I call "The GOOF Principle" A practical and easy way to catch yourself before ending up like Jonah who found himself in an unpleasant place as a result of a bitter heart.

_G_et over yourself!

_O_wn your mess!

_O_pen up

_F_orgive yourself!

This principle will be the real application of what we discover through Jonah's story. It applies to us in such a relevant way, that I believe it can help you start to become the person God knows you to be. The real you! Oh, by the way, God loves the real you, not the one you are pretending to be or the one you think He demands you be like. You see, one falsehood we have believed in the church and in our culture today is that we have to make ourselves into something likeable and good before God or anyone else will love us. It's impossible to achieve because no one is good enough. Or as the Bible says, " we all fall short".

So, when we stop pretending and own the messes we make, we have the opportunity to get back up and try again.

The hardest part of **"The GOOF Principle"** is forgiving yourself for falling short. (We'll tackle that subject later) You might be wondering why it is so easy to find ourselves in these sticky situations. If you are anything like me, you have probably asked yourself this question; "How did I end up this mess....again?" Many of us are constantly running om God and ourselves and don't even realize we are doing . God may be desperately trying to get our attention, but e are too busy rationalizing and compartmentalizing our ves. We, like Jonah are being swallowed up by the giant fish at swim in our world. Giant fish that look a lot like debt, ddictions, bad relationships, and a life marked by just getting y. God wants us to live life to the full but we have traded is way for our way. Our definition of a full life is no where ear what God has in mind, and I am convinced He will se all means necessary to get our attention. The question ecomes are we willing to stop running and start listening?

Trust me when I say that you can try as many self-help chniques as you want, and sign up for life coaches for each ay of the week. You can eat all the right foods, and mix ilates with Yoga while watching Dr. Phil. It doesn't matter. your heart is hard when it comes to understanding God's race and love for all people, then there is trouble on the high as ahead.

Section I: "The GOOF Principle"

Get Over Yourself

James 4: 13-14

Now, listen you who say, "Today or tomorrow we will go to this or that city, spend a year there, carry on business and make money." Why, you don't even know what will happen tomorrow. What is your life? You are a mist that appears for a little while and then vanishes. (NIV)

James 4: 13-14

And now I have a word for you who brashly announce, "Today—at the latest, tomorrow—we're off to such and such a city for the year. We're going to start a business and make a lot of money." You don't know the first thing about tomorrow. You're nothing but a wisp of fog, catching a brief bit of sun before disappearing. (The Message)

It starts with the *in your face* realization that we give ourselves way too much credit. I mean seriously, if you stop long enough to think about all the bone-head things you've ever done, said, or thought…..wow!

Step one is hard…

Get over yourself

O

O

F

Chapter 1

My Story - My Fish

I wrestled with whether or not to share my personal story and how I came to surrender my life to Jesus Christ. I considered several reasons for why I thought it wouldn't be a good idea. For example, if I share too much personal information then you might think I'm one of those people who is trying to capitalize on the struggles I have encountered. Or, you might just say to yourself, "Hey, I'm not as messed up as that guy so I guess I'm okay." Both of these are wrong, of course, because at some level we are all dysfunctional.

The bottom line is this: I decided to share parts of my life because one of the most powerful ways God reveals Himself is through our weakness. Every time I go somewhere to speak and share my story full of GOOFS and how God has made something good out of it, I always have people tell me how much it has encouraged them. More importantly, people feel connected to God in a way they haven't felt for a long time. God can use anyone to accomplish His purposes. Our job is to not hide behind the façade of having it all together.

Life before Jesus

I'll share my story in two parts because I don't have any idea where you are in your relationship with God. I hate when people assume something as important as your relationship to

Christ. You might be reading this book and thinking about your relationship to God and how you are not sure where you stand. Maybe you are a Christian who has been in church for years but your heart has become somewhat bitter because you feel disconnected from God. You may be desperate for a touch from Him and reading my story may cause a spark that could set you on fire for Him all over again. I pray so.

From the time I took my first drink of alcohol at age 15, I knew nothing about how my brain was wired. I just knew I liked the feeling. I will interject early in this story that I have two of the most wonderful parents a child could ever ask for. They were on to me at an early age and tried over and over again to get my attention about the dangers of drinking. It's not their fault. I was good at concealing things. I became a master at manipulating circumstances and diverting attention. I was a professional con man by age 16 and all I cared about was having a good time and being the life of the party. I would always drink to excess because I didn't understand why there was any reason not to. This behavior became addictive and followed me into my college years. I was functioning but just barely. I won't go into details about how bad it got, because most of my friends and family have probably suffered in some way as a result of my struggles. All I can tell you is sometime around age 23, I knew I had a huge problem.

I stumbled through my 20's and into my early 30's literally and emotionally. I was trying so hard to be inconspicuous and just be normal like everyone else, but down deep I knew alcohol had me beat. I had begun to dread the weekend because I knew what was coming. You see, I had rationalized that because I could hold off from drinking between Monday and Thursday that somehow I was not an alcoholic and I could let it all loose on the weekend. As I got older, this really took its toll on my health. I would drink enough on Friday and Saturday that my hangover would last until Tuesday. So, basically by Wednesday I felt good, and Thursday I felt great! I felt so good by Thursday that I was ready to party again on Friday. The cycle was horrible. I could not escape it.

Then, God in His grace gave me a moment of clarity. I had been to church off and on as a kid, and my grandmother and several others I know were praying for me all my life. I knew God but I didn't KNOW God. I was running from Him even though I desperately wanted to be right with Him. Another vicious cycle I could not escape. When He gave me a moment of clarity on a drive home from Chicago, I could see clearly long enough to know He was reaching out to me. I know now, He was gently speaking into my spirit saying… " Jay you are an alcoholic…..and I love you….and I'm wanting to come into your heart".

I felt so much peace, and at the same time, I was scared to let Him in. I didn't want to go to rehab, and I didn't want anyone to know what I was feeling. I just wanted everything to be made right. God spoke these two words into my spirit, "Trust Me."

I can tell you that not long after that moment of clarity, God led me to a church and began speaking deep into my heart. I had not quit drinking yet, but I was realizing for the first time that I had a hope. Let me be clear, I didn't think I had hope......I realized that I had "A" Hope and His name was Jesus.

> I was tired of operating out of my own strength. I was empty inside and God just kept whispering in my ear, "Trust Me."

Romans 10:11

As the Scripture says, "Anyone who trusts in him will never be put to shame."

(NIV)

I went to meet with Pastor Jim Lyon, whom God had been using to speak into my life at a level I didn't know possible. I had rehearsed something in my head to say but when I opened my mouth nothing came out. But the tears did. I cried a lot, and he smiled a lot. He was witnessing first hand God's transformation of my life. I'm sure he never gets tired of seeing that. I shared with him my desire to know Jesus and be baptized. I came up out of the water the next week in front of about 800 people in the congregation. There were several people in the congregation who have known me for years and I'm sure they were wondering if the end of the world was near when they saw me standing there, freshly dripping with the symbolic remnants of a new life in Jesus Christ. I can only imagine what they were probably thinking but I knew what I was experiencing was real, and that's all that mattered to me.

Life with Jesus

It's been close to 10 years since I gave my heart to Jesus and was baptized. He **Delivered** me from alcohol **Instantly!** Did you comprehend what I just said? It's powerful, so just think about it for a minute. When we think of God in our culture, we often forget how powerful He is. We underestimate Him, and I'm telling you He does not like it. We need to recapture a sense of Awe when we think about God and believe He can and will work in powerful ways for His sake, and our good.

Now, for those of you who might be thinking… "Well, maybe you really didn't have a problem with alcohol because it sounds too corny to believe God delivered you"…let me give you a glimpse of my life at the time;

When I was 16, I really started liking alcohol and the way it made me feel. It was becoming a priority. From age 16 to 18 partying on the weekends was becoming more and more consistent and my addictive patterns were fueling the fire and igniting a self-destructive life style. From the age 19 on, I would drink at least 18-20 beers from Friday afternoon through the early hours of Saturday morning. Often there were nights when beer just wouldn't do the trick and I would revert to hard liquor, and when that stopped tasting good, then it would be back to beer. It was a well known fact, that by my early 20's I would always drink to excess and end up if not passed out, then at the very least incoherent. I could tell you stories….. but you wouldn't believe them. The crazy thing is, I did seem to be managing my life in somewhat of a productive manner.

I mean I could still hold a job and function but increasingly I was becoming someone that I was ashamed of, and other people were starting to avoid. Blackouts, drinking to cure hang-overs, and a never ending appetite to kill the pain was my life. What was the pain? A life without God. I didn't know it at the time, but my pain was mostly because I felt I had no purpose and I didn't know why. By the time I had reached my early 30's, I was a slave to alcohol. I hated it but I knew it was my master. I was really beginning to hurt those that I love and now I had two small children counting on me to be a dad. I was in way over my head and I was scared.

Like I said, it's been close to 10 years since I gave my heart and life to Jesus Christ and I have not a drink since that day…. April 19th 1999. God took it away. Isn't that AWESOME!

He also delivered me from cigarettes and swearing. (for the most part) I still wear socks and sandals, drink way too much coffee, and have a warped sense of humor, but I've got all eternity to work on that! People often ask me why God will do that for some but not all and I don't have a good answer except to say, when you really surrender everything into His control, He is powerful and able to do the impossible. He accomplishes His purposes, His way. Never forget that. All I can tell you is that He's real, and He loves you, and He wants your heart. I thank Him often for setting me free from my sin, alcohol, and other destructive behaviors and I also am constantly learning that I'm most thankful for who He is. He's *"IT"* There is nothing more important than knowing what life is all about, and if you stop long enough to hear Him and to let Him in, you'll discover that life is about Him. Life starts with Him, is sustained by Him, and our meaning is all in Him.

I found my story in the book of Jonah, because I realized for the first time that the FISH was not the punishment but the provision of God. I was definitely running from God, causing storms and hanging out in unpleasant places. He used it however to penetrate my heart and show His Love, Forgiveness, and Grace and when I surrendered to Him, out of the FISH I came. I came out with a message, and the message is…. "It starts with our hearts."

My prayer is that you read this book and see God in a new light. It's not a fad or a trendy new age thing I'm promoting. Everything I experienced is biblical and I encourage you to search your heart and listen to it. I want you to know that the God who created you and loves you more than you can imagine. If you are searching for meaning in your life and want to know why you keep ending up inside the fish, my prayer is that you wake up and realize God sent the fish, because He wants your heart.

My life has not been easy since giving it to Christ, but it does have purpose. I will always be striving for new and relevant ways to share God's love with people as long as He allows. But sometimes I *"GOOF"*……….and so will you. Let's figure out how to handle it when we do.

Chapter 2

Discovering the Jonah in All of Us.

Do you ever feel like you're running from something?

Have you been pretending for so long, that you don't even know who you are anymore?

Are you tired of **Struggling, Searching, and Suffering?**

Are you ready to GET OUT OF YOUR FISH?

That's what this book is all about. Whether you consider yourself religious, slightly spiritual, or you only go to church so you can play on the softball team, this book is for you. The story of Jonah in the Bible is one most people have probably heard of but may misinterpret. You would only have had to go to church a few times as a kid to hear the story in a Sunday school class and even if you never went to a church service in your life, you probably have some working knowledge of the story of Jonah. If you have a Bible.....read the book of Jonah to refresh your memory. If you don't have a Bible, go online and find a resource that you can use to read it. It's only 4 chapters and it might just change your life!

I think it is safe to assume that if you read the book of Jonah, the first conclusion you'd come to is that Jonah messed up big time! He rebelled, did not obey and so God punished him by having a huge fish swallow him. This pattern of belief reinforces the way most people have grown up being taught to think about God. Their view of Him is bent towards strictness, rules, wrath, punishment, etc... etc... Yes, God is Holy and has principles we need to live by and if we don't, there are consequences, but how we view God needs to change. Yes, Jonah ran from God. Yes, God sent a fish. Yes, things got ugly for awhile. But.......

Have you ever stopped long enough to consider that the FISH was the *provision* of God?

The Fish is where Jonah came to terms with *his* poor heart condition.

The Fish is where Jonah *found* God again.

The Fish is where Jonah found his *purpose* again.

The Fish is what *saved* Jonah.

Are you in a fish? Have you ever looked at your circumstances and thought... "How did I get myself into this, and better yet how am I going to get out of it?" The real question should be... "Am I ready to get over it, and get on with my life?"

I can tell you this-- When you truly start to understand that God loves you, unconditionally, and wants you to **Get**

Out Of the Fish, then your sense of purpose in this life will forever be changed. If you really want out, be prepared, because the fish you are in is feeling queasy and is about to vomit you right back onto your feet so you can change the world.

As you continue reading, you will start to see it's about HIM. It's about God's plans not ours. However, He does want you involved and He does have something for you to do, so we need to really let some things sink in: He loves us. He loves YOU! He loves your neighbor who mows the lawn in dark socks and sandals. He loves people at the drive-thru who, even though there are nine people in your car, always seem to forget your food only. He loves the people who tailgate you as they drive down the road and most of all He loves the opposing team. What? Yes, it's true. God does love whatever team it is that you hate. Get over it.

> I always thought it was confusing when an athlete would come out and say things like "I just thank God for our victory today. The good Lord was really with us and without Him we couldn't have done it." Does this mean God doesn't love the other team? What if it was the Green Bay Packers? Are you telling me God doesn't love the Packers? I always picture a guy with a worn out Brett Favre jersey on, sitting in his chair with a bowl of cheese in his lap asking his wife, … "Why doesn't God like the Packers anymore?"

The Jonah in All of Us

You can probably walk into any church in North America and ask people what they think the book of Jonah is all about. I have done this myself and I have no doubt you would get the same response as I did. For the most part it always goes something like this:

"The story of Jonah is about disobedience and how Jonah was punished because he didn't obey God's commands. He suffered for three days in a huge fish and then God gave him a second chance. Everything turned out okay in the end but we must remember to obey God, or else."

This, of course, is the "cliff notes" version and it does cover the basics, but when we leave it right there we're missing the real story. The book of Jonah in the Bible is a love story. God loves Jonah. God also loves the people in a land called Nineveh that He told Jonah to go to. He gave Jonah a big responsibility to carry out a mission that would reveal God's grace and love to a people who were considered to be evil and far from God in their hearts. Upon receiving this assignment from God, Jonah ran from God and what unfolds thereafter, is a love story illustrating God's grace, forgiveness, through the means of a storm, a giant fish, and an entire city that gives themselves over to God.

So, why do we miss the point so often when we talk about Jonah in the Bible? One reason perhaps is we still don't read it enough, and for that matter, the Old Testament in general is not something most people cozy up to by the fire for a nice relaxing evening of feel good reading. I think we miss the point sometimes because we start with a wrong viewpoint of God. The story of Jonah is most often told early on in Sunday School at a young age. It's an easy lesson to grab onto as a kid because of the basic message of right and wrong, not to mention the entertainment factor of the story itself. Think about it, there's adventure on the high seas, storms, and someone getting thrown overboard. Then throw in a giant fish, and some vomit.....kids love it! The problem is once the message of disobedience, punishment, and God's wrath are repeatedly drilled into the minds of our youth, it's hard for them to unlearn this view of God's character. Don't misunderstand, there are always consequences for the choices we make in life and if we choose to ignore God, we are making a grave mistake but focusing more on His love and less on wrath will help us understand the Jonah in all of us.

Most of the people I've talked with about the book of Jonah have in one way or another summed it up by reiterating what we already know...*obey or else!* This leads to a legalistic viewpoint and spills over into our churches, homes, and more dangerously our hearts. I would argue this mindset (which is very common) usually starts with good intentions but ends up making Christians more judgmental of others, bitter, and arrogantly insulated from God's own heart. I certainly don't want to live my life being bitter and ineffective, and my guess is you don't either. So, then the question becomes... "What do we do?" Let's start with an honest reflection of how we view God, how He views us, and then see if we can uncover the Jonah in all of us.

In Chip Ingram's book **<u>GOD: As He Longs For You to See Him</u>** (which I highly recommend you read after reading my book of course) he lays out a way for us to change our paradigms in the way we view God. More importantly, how God views us! One of my favorite principles from the book is:

*"What you think about God shapes your whole relationship with him. In addition, what you believe God thinks about **you** determines how close you will grow toward him.*

Here's the point. If we keep on running around ***trying*** to please God and in the process we are stepping all over other people's hearts, then not only do we have a jaded view of God, but we have missed the love story of how God views all people. Make no mistake, there is a little Jonah in all of us. (Maybe more than you think) We all hang on to our viewpoints and judgments of others until God breaks down those barriers. Sometimes, it's easy for God to get our attention. Other times, He gets creative. Creative to God may be painful to us, and it may even come in the form of a giant fish. But REMEMBER THIS......the "Fish" was the PROVISION not the punishment. The fish is the only thing that made it possible to reconnect with God. Jonah would have drown and been lost forever, if God had not sent that fish. God rescued Jonah even though he had run away and although I'm sure Jonah would have preferred a Helicopter and a rope, it turned out to be the perfect place for redemption. Are you starting to get a new view of God? Is your perspective changing? Look at your circumstances right now and determine if you might be inside a fish of your own. Maybe you have been in one before, or maybe there's one swimming your way right now. It's all about our heart, and God's desire to get our attention. Trust me, HE loves you. Even though there is a Jonah somewhere inside of you….HE loves you.

Chapter 3

Stop Running

I am a serious movie buff. Not so much that I've seen every movie ever made, but it's more like I can quote lines from almost any movie I have seen. I also like to relate my life's situations through movies. Most men have this ability and love to quote movie lines to each other as a way of communicating. It must be a cultural thing relating to the times we live in coupled with the fact that most guys don't like to talk about anything deep or meaningful when they're with other guys. Women have never understood why men love to quote movie lines to each other, but I'm sure they discuss it often when they go to the bathroom together!

Not only does God use movies to stir my spirit and keep me in touch with the culture, but He has wired me in a way that allows me to use movies (and music) to help others see God's character. We are talking about Jonah and the fact that there is a Jonah in all of us. We all end up in some sort of fish from time to time, and as I read the story of Jonah in the Bible, it doesn't take long to uncover where things start to go wrong:

Jonah 1:1-3

The word of the Lord came to Jonah son of Amittai: "Go to the great city of Nineveh and preach against it, because its wickedness has come up before me." But Jonah ran away from the Lord and headed for Tarshish.

Now, you're saying, "What does this have to do with movies?" When I read the above scripture, I instantly get a picture in my head and it looks something like Forrest Gump running down a dirt road at full speed with the "Jennay" in the distance yelling, "run Forrest....run!" Okay, okay, maybe you don't see things the way I do, but the point is most people believe Jonah got the call and bolted in the other direction at full speed. Not true. This is an area we need to explore if we are going to take the steps necessary in getting out of the fish we may be in. Running from God can be done slowly, methodically, and sometimes we never even have to go anywhere.

Rationalized Running

Jonah ran from God. There is no disputing it, nor is there any way to justify it. The dude wasn't thinking clearly. Or was he? We all have this image of Jonah running out of fear and that God must have been in high pursuit right behind him. Was Jonah ducking in and out of alleyways and hiding in caves hoping to give God the slip? It was nothing like that at all. It was a choice, then a plan, followed by a nap.

The Bible says:

Jonah 1:3b

He went down to Joppa, where he found a ship bound for that port. After paying the fare, he went aboard and sailed for Tarshish to flee from the Lord. (NIV)

Jonah decided to go his own way. It would have been a substantial distance for Jonah to travel to get from where he was to Joppa. On top of that, he boarded a ship that was heading the opposite way from where God wanted him to go. Jonah had time as he traveled to Joppa to think about what he was doing. Yes, he was fleeing but it wasn't in desperation or in a full sprint. It was slow and steady and much like we do today. I'll bet there was some rationalizing going on inside his head. Remember, Jonah was a prophet and he knew God very well. A prophet's job, so to speak, is to carry out God's commands and to warn and inform people about what will come to pass in relation to God's plan. If people are not in relationship with God, then a prophet's mission is to get them to understand the importance of putting God first and everything else second. Jonah knew how all of this was supposed to work, so why did he run? It was his heart. For some reason, Jonah's heart was in a very bitter and judgmental condition towards those nasty people who lived in Nineveh. He didn't want to go because at some level he thought they did not deserve God's grace. Let the rationalization begin!!

If we fast forward to today, we will find that this type of running from God not only still exists, but is being done at a whole new level. *Rationalized Running* is a deceptive trap many people fall into over the course of their lives. It applies to all people whether you call yourself a Christian or not. It can be defined as a term I use to describe people (myself included) who on the "outside" appear to have it all together. They always seem busy, they always seem to be going somewhere, but down deep in their hearts they are simply running from something. The rationalization part comes in when we become masters of running from God without anyone else noticing. We can get our lives looking really good on the outside and other people's perception of us is stellar, but it could all be a way of running or hiding from a relationship with God that needs attention. You can find this most often in church (sad but true) and people can run from God by rationalizing all the "things" they do for Him. The church is filled with people (including myself from time to time) that appear to have it all together and serve in many areas, but whose hearts are in a full out sprint in the opposite direction that God wants them to go.

Hosea 6:6

"I'm after love that lasts, not more religion. I want you to know God, not go to more prayer meetings." (The Message)

Jonah ran, paid his fare, and boarded the ship. He thought everything was under control. Many of us get up, go to church, and pay our tithes and offerings. We also assume we have things under control. But I challenge you to check your heart, and see if there are areas in need of a fresh perspective from God. The only way God can get there is if you let Him in. One of the barriers that we create along as we run and rationalize is a perception of us that gets built up over time. If we appear to have it all together long enough, then we start to believe it ourselves. We categorize people in the church and turn them into icons based on things such as who serves the most or who can quote scripture the best. We label people in the church who teach Sunday school or can pray well as "good Christians", then we all try to live up to that perception of what we need to do. This takes the place of our relationship with God and slowly we start to rationalize and run from the things that really matter to God. (Loving God, Loving Others) There are several "labels" in the Christian world that add fuel to the fire of perception, and over time, do real damage. Here is one my favorites:

Sometimes people refer to a person in the church as a "Strong Christian" WHAT DOES THAT MEAN????? Do they lift weights? Do they rip phone books in half during Bible study? Maybe they like to arm wrestle while laying hands on people. I'm not being flip about this, (okay maybe a little), but the sooner we all lay down our "labels" the sooner we can stop working so hard to maintain them.

Start Reflecting More

Maybe you are not running from anything. Maybe you have a great relationship with God and others but your life is still in a state of constant disarray simply because of where you are at in your life. Work is busy, home life is busy, the kids, TIVO, YOGA, food, water; breathing….etc….it all takes its toll. It has always been my contention that we need to slow down long enough everyday to reflect on our lives and our relationship to God. Reflection is a lost art these days, especially in the U.S. If I asked one of my kids about reflecting they would assume I was talking about a mirror. No matter if you are running from something or not, we all need to stop and reflect more. I believe if we get quiet for just a few minutes each day, it doesn't take long for us think about the important things in life. If God can just get us quiet long enough to start working on our hearts, then real change can happen. The problem is, as we start to look inward it quickly becomes uncomfortable and we suddenly remember today was the day we were going to start flossing our teeth more and we'd better get to it! Thus the slow, methodical running from God continues. To actually slow down long enough, to see what God sees and to hear what He wants us to hear, we must be intentional. We must also begin to truly understand our need of Him. Again, whether you have been a Christian for years or you are searching for some meaning in your life, please understand God loves you just as you are. I know it's scary to let Him in. I realize the human tendency is to run and try to protect areas that no one else knows about but I've got news for you.....He already knows everything. We must allow the Lord, our Creator, to penetrate areas of our heart with His Love, Grace, and Forgiveness.

> Keep asking yourself a question:
> "How bad do I want out of this fish?"
> If you are serious about understanding who God is, why you are where you are, and how He wants to get you out.....then you must let Him fully into your heart.

Psalm 9: 9-10

The Lord is a refuge for the oppressed, and stronghold in times of trouble. Those who know your name will trust in you, for you Lord have never forsaken those who seek you. (NIV)

As scary as it is for us we must stop running *from* God and start running *to* Him.

<u>Chapter 4</u>

Me and God At Starbuck's

Having established that God is always interested more in our hearts and an ongoing relationship with us, the question becomes… "Are you willing?" Jonah had a relationship with God because he was a prophet, but when it came time to engage in that relationship by doing what God asked, Jonah refused. To really be engaged with God, we must be honest with Him, and more importantly, with ourselves. One way to do that is to start reading His word with a different perspective.

"Me and God Syndrome" is a term I came up with to describe people who somehow believe they are on the same playing field with God. They think they have Him all figured out and they don't mind telling people about it! Even if you read the Bible everyday and spend time in prayer, you can have the "Me and God Syndrome". (I know, because I'm recovering from it at the moment!) I know sometimes as I read God's word, I have an attitude that I'm so much smarter than the people in the Bible. As I read, in my head I'm thinking… "Wow, I would never be that stubborn Lord, I mean seriously, how stupid can some of these people be?" **It's as if me and God are sitting at Starbuck's sipping a Latte' and discussing how some people never learn.** Unfortunately, that is how most professing Christians think, go to church, and experience their religious life, and its flat wrong.

Isaiah 29:13

The Lord says:

"These people come near me with their mouth and honor me with their lips, but their hearts are far from me. Their worship of me is made up only of rules taught by men." (NIV)

How can we avoid this type of thinking?

Try this:

Imagine God is currently writing Volume II of the bible, and guess who's starring in one of the main books? Yep, it's you! God's new volume will be released in about 100 years and He's going to write about the life you are living right now.

"The book of_____" (Insert your name)

So, for the next 30 days what would you like God to write about? Will you be remembered as:

1. Stubborn
2. Prideful
3. Someone God used as an example of how not to live
4. Judgmental

OR

1. A person after God's heart
2. Humble- A seeker of God's kingdom
3. Genuine, Faithful
4. Merciful, Forgiving

I guess the real question is, in 100 years will someone be sitting at a Starbuck's reading about you saying, "Wow, how stubborn can you be?"

Fresh Perspective

Many professing Christians do not spend enough time being engaged with God by reading the Bible with an open heart and mind. There are many who have simply grown up in church and have believed in Jesus, but don't ever get engaged in a dynamic relationship with Him. They may have perfect attendance on Sunday, give financially, and have a Jesus fish on the back of every car they own, but there is a disconnect in how they interact with God and others. Jonah paid his fare, boarded a ship, and went below deck to fall asleep. He was asleep to his surroundings, and asleep to the needs of the people God wanted Jonah to reach out to. Jonah thought he knew better how to dole out Godly justice, because in his mind, those awful people in Nineveh did not deserve God's forgiveness.

The moment Jonah decided he knew more than God was the same moment a Giant Fish was headed in his direction. I believe many people in churches today are asleep and don't even know it. They are below deck sleeping soundly, even as the storms start to kick up all around them. I include myself in this category because no one is above falling into this mindset. Pride is such a destructive, evil thing in our lives and it's often disguised as "discernment". When we judge others based on the outside appearance of their lives and quickly surmise what that person needs to do in order to satisfy our definition of being a Christian....we are in dangerous waters. This isn't discernment, nor discipling. It is not even close to being reaching out in love to help. It's the Me and God Syndrome, plain and simple. Let me put some meat on this bone for you; it's what turns people away from the church in droves. Christians are very good about slipping into this mentality and it shows by the way we often try and force people into a religion instead of loving them into a relationship.

Luke 18: 9-14

He (Jesus) told his next story to some who were complacently pleased with themselves over their moral performance and looked down their noses at the common people: "Two men went up to the Temple to pray, one a Pharisee, the other a tax man. (In Jesus' day the Pharisee would be the equivalent to a devout religious person. The tax men of those days were notoriously dishonest and sinful)

The Pharisee posed and prayed like this: 'Oh, God, I thank you that I am not like other people—robbers, crooks, adulterers, or heaven forbid like this tax man. I fast twice a week and tithe on all my income.' "Meanwhile the tax man slumped in the shadows, his face in his hands, not daring to look up, said, 'God give mercy. Forgive me, a sinner.'" Jesus commented, "This tax man, not the other, went home made right with God. If you walk around with your nose in the air, you're going to end up flat on your face, but if you're content to be simply yourself, you will become more than yourself." (The Message)

Jonah made the mistake of deciding who was good enough for God's love and forgiveness and so do we. Jonah ultimately ended up inside a fish, and like Jonah if we continue to run, sleep, and judge our way through life you can bet God is lining up a whole school of fish just for us. Remember, the Giant Fish was the provision of God. It was the only way Jonah could come to terms with his poor attitude and lack of mercy for others. It was the only place that he remembered that all things center around God and His unbelievable plan for our lives. Are you identifying any fish in your life yet?

Prayer

One way to combat the Me and God Syndrome is to spend time praying. Earlier, we called this reflection. Either way, it's all about putting God first and slowing down long enough to hear Him. It should always result with us coming away with a sense of surrender and contentment. We surrender through prayer because we realize our dependence upon God, and hopefully, we come away content because God has shown us that He is all we need.

John Piper, author of "**Desiring God**" says this:

Any servant who tries to get off the divine dole and strike up a manly partnership with his heavenly Master is in revolt against the Creator.

Good service is always and fundamentally receiving mercy, not rendering assistance.

Those of us who run from God like Jonah did, in a very

calculated way, do so because we have rationalized our way into thinking we are on the same level of God's thinking.

God does not need our help, HE wants our heart. If HE has our heart, we have purpose.

We all must come to terms with our own individual hearts and the areas that God is speaking to us about. The best way to start is to come clean, give it all to Him, and ask that He would search the heart.

Fall in love with Jesus, who is the lover of your soul, and do whatever you have to do to wake yourself up from the arrogant nap you're taking. Quit rationalizing, stop running, and for heaven's sake...GET OVER YOURSELF!

> God does not need our help, HE wants our heart. If HE has our heart, we have purpose.

Section II: "The GOOF Principle"

Own Your Mess

Psalm 32: 3-5

When I kept silent my bones wasted away through my groaning all day long. For day and night your hand was heavy upon me; my strength was sapped as in the heat of summer.

Then I acknowledged my sin to you and did not cover up my iniquity. I said "I will confess my transgressions to the Lord" and you forgave the guilt of my sin. (NIV)

If you have gotten over yourself (at least for the moment) and realize you desperately want to get out of the fish you are in, it's time to own your mess. Jonah had to, and so do we. I really don't want to sugar coat this part of the GOOF principle, because when you own your mess, you must own it completely. There can be no pointing fingers, no whining, and no more hiding from God. Once you come to terms with this part of the process, you are on your way to being spit out onto dry land, and ready to change the world!

Take inventory: Are you over yourself? Good! Let's move on.

Get over yourself...

Own your mess...

O

F

Chapter 5

Pride Does Come Before the Fall

I'm notorious for getting myself into sticky situations. (My own Fish) Some are serious, but most are humorous. The point being, usually it's my ego or pride that gets things started. It's a constant reminder to me that God really wants me to get over myself, and the importance I put on the perception I desire others to have of me. In short, I crave acceptance, and sometimes that leads to a false pride or a built up ego just for show.

God doesn't like either of those things.

Proverbs 16: 18

Pride goes before destruction, a haughty spirit before a fall. (NIV)

My favorite version of this scripture comes from "The Message" which says it this way;

"First pride, then the crash- the bigger the ego, the harder the fall."

I was in Vail, Colorado at a sales conference for the company I was working for at the time. I was really excited to reconnect with an associate who I had trained with. He lived in San Diego and would always ask me how I could stand to live in Indiana where there was nothing to do but watch the corn grow. (ouch) He would always rub it in because where he lived it was a short drive to the beach and in a few hours he could be in the mountains skiing. I would do my best to make Indiana an adventurous place to live when I described it to him, but He never bought it.

We met in Colorado and had a few laughs and then the jabs started coming about living in a cornfield. I quickly defended myself the best I could and then he offered to teach me how to ski. (Since, in his mind I was from Indiana and therefore only capable of driving a tractor.) I informed him I knew how to ski and I'd meet him on the slopes the next morning.

Now, I'd been skiing only once in my life on a slope that was used to teach beginners. I would put myself into a crouch and rocket myself down to the bottom and crash to stop. This was my only experience on the slopes and now my ego and my big mouth had me headed for a slice of humble pie.

I met my friend David the next morning and we got on the ski lift. He asked again, point blank, "Are you sure you can handle these slopes?" It was my last chance to bow out, but my pride wouldn't let me. As we rode up on the lift together, I was in awe of the beauty that surrounded us. The mountains were breathtaking and the views were indescribable. God certainly does reveal Himself through the creation, because it was just so beautiful and all I wanted to do was continue to take it all in. This was about the time God reminded me….. "Jay, you're in over your head."

The ski lift just kept going higher. I was in awe and I was starting to feel like I did in school when we would have a pop quiz and I was not prepared. We were so high on the mountain; I expected to receive an oxygen device and guidance from a Sherpa. This was no joke! I managed to get off the lift and not look stupid, but I could tell David was starting to have his doubts about me.

I made my way to the starting point and David said, "See you at the bottom!" My first thought was yeah, you'll see me alright….being loaded into an ambulance with a ski pole sticking out of an unnamed body part!

As I saw my good friend David swooshing back and forth and getting farther and farther away, I decided it was now or never. I summoned up some courage and took off. In the first fifty yards, I fell four times. I fell fast, and I fell hard. It hurt. I was hearing God whispering, "What in the world are you trying to prove?" Now, I've always believed God has a sense of humor, but what happened next was borderline cruel and unusual punishment when it comes to Divine Justice. David was gone and probably already at the bottom of the hill. If I didn't get down there soon, he would start to wonder and worry, so I made a decision to get down the only way I knew how. I took off my skis and tucked them under one arm. I took my ski poles and tucked them under the other arm and began to slide down the hill on my you know what. The whole time I'm thinking about how I get myself in these situations and how humiliated I always feel. I was asking God to help me get down the hill as quickly as possible and if He could limit the embarrassment factor as much as possible. What I found out was that the most humiliating part was yet to come and I think God got a big kick out of it.

I had stopped half way down to rest my back side and to make sure I was burning a hole in my snowsuit. As I sit there taking a breather and wiping the snot from my face, a little girl no more than about 10 years old came swooshing by, stopped on a dime, and said, "Sir, are you okay? I can have a rescue unit sent up for you if you'd like." Yep, God had sent a child to shove in the last bit of my foot that wasn't already in my mouth. She was so cute and polite that it made me sick to my stomach. I could tell she had a genuine concern for my wellbeing, something that was truly innocent a pure. I contemplated making up a story about hurting my knee and somehow saving what little pride I had left, but I just smiled and said… "I'll be fine." God knew the point had been made. My mouth and my pride had gotten me high on a mountain, and my humility and my backside were the only things that could get me down.

Pride can get us into situations that may turn into humorous stories over time, but more often than not pride robs us of living life to the fullest. Pride will always put a barrier between you and God and the outcome over time will not be pleasant. God hates pride, and I can tell you that pride is something I struggle with to this day. Let's keep this in the right perspective, though, because I don't want you to think that God hates you because you might be struggling with pride.

God hates pride; not you

God loves you; not your pride

Chapter 6

How Can You Sleep at A Time Like This?

Jonah had boarded the ship, gone below deck, and checked out. There was no wake up call, no agenda for the next day planned, nor did he really care. I'm guessing Jonah wanted to be left alone, because he was below deck and isolated from the rest of the people on the ship. If you think about it, Jonah is a lot like us or vice versa because when we are running from something and our hearts are closed off, so is everything else. We just want to be in our own world where we think it is safe and sound. We want to be in a place where we think we are in control and that nobody will suspect anything.

Proverbs 14:12

There is a way that seems right to a man, but in the end it leads to death.

One of the hardest things to do is admit there is something wrong in your life or in your heart. I'll even go one step further, saying it's difficult to admit that you are wrong about anything, even something small. **Example: Men & Driving Directions... Enough said!** In fact, it's so hard that we usually try anything and everything to avoid even thinking about taking full responsibility. I'm always wary of someone who finds ease in admitting their faults on a regular basis. People who always want to "take full responsibility" usually are just paying lip service and are operating out of a false humility. The fact is, their hearts haven't changed a bit..... and deep down they really don't think they are wrong.

We see this phenomenon in our culture today with professional athletes and other famous people. It's not that these are the only people who mess up and then have to own it, but they are highly visible and end up in our living rooms on T.V. almost every night. The cycle goes something like this: A famous athlete or movie star finds themselves in a compromising situation. They do something illegal or stupid and get caught. (I wonder if we just made being stupid illegal...?) Then, a publicist writes an apology for the person, schedules a press conference, and we hear something like this:

"I would like to first apologize to my fans for this unfortunate incident. We all make mistakes and I am only human. If I have offended anyone then I am sorry. I take full responsibility for my actions."

Translation: I'm sorry this has put my image in jeopardy. I got caught....I'll be craftier next time. If you are put off by my actions, I don't understand why. I have a great lawyer who will get me out of this.

Why? The question is why we all fight so hard to hold

on to a belief or a behavior when we know it is wrong? My answer is simple. We are STUBBORN! First, we run like the wind. Then, we hold on for dear life to what we think is right. Just because we "take full responsibility" in words only, doesn't mean anything has changed.

Jonah 1: 4-6

Then the Lord sent a great wind on the sea, and such a violent storm arose that the ship threatened to break up. All the sailors were afraid and each cried out to his own god. And they threw the cargo into the sea to lighten the ship. But Jonah had gone below deck, where he lay down and fell into a deep sleep. The captain went to him and said, "How can you sleep?"

When there are storms raging about in our life, are we even considering that it might be of our own doing? I know that Christians like to play the "Enemy" card when things are going bad. What I mean is that too often our first response to problems, or storms in our life are blamed on the Devil. It's easy to claim that we, as spiritual people are under attack and we need people, to pray for us. We shouldn't discount the mischief that the Devil is conjuring up, but we don't need to give him too much credit either.

1 Peter 2: 19-20

What counts is that you put up with it for God's sake when you're treated badly for no good reason. There's no particular virtue in accepting punishment that you well deserve. (The Message)

If there are storms raging in your life, and you are still asleep in your denial, just know that God is patient....very, very patient.

NASCAR Christian

Maybe you're suffering from something I like to call "Nascar Christian Disease". The symptoms are:

1. Saying all the right things (sound-bites)
2. Changing the subject to make yourself look good
3. Denying what is actually going on all around you, even though everyone else knows the truth.
4. Convincing yourself you actually have everything under control and are about to do something great with your life.

NASCAR drivers are the best at this and I'm sure we have picked up some of their traits along the way. They can have the worst race of their career and make it sound like they were about to win the race. It usually goes something like this.

Reporter: "What happened out there, are you okay?"

Driver: "Not sure, it wasn't my fault though, I can tell you that. I was holding my line and it's just a shame someone hit me because we had a car that could win the race!"

Reporter: "But you were 14 laps down and all by yourself. It looks like you wrecked all by yourself."

Driver: "No, no, no…. someone definitely hit me or something. We had a great car and I was just about to make my move. The Chevy, ABC Company, XYZ Company, BBQ number 99 was real impressive today until someone wrecked us.

Reporter: "It looked like on your last pit stop someone forgot to put on all the tires. Could that have been the cause of your wreck….all by yourself….14 laps down?

Driver: "No, that was just something we were trying to see if it would make the car run better. It was working, because I was really making a run for the front.

  Have you convinced yourself you are okay in your relationship to God and others, even though down deep you know you are not? The storms are raging and God is trying to get your attention, but you are sound asleep. Sleep walking, sleep talking, and constantly dreaming of the day when things will change.

Things like….

Debt

Addiction

Adultery

Workaholic

Pornography

Gangs/Violence

Loveless marriages

However we got there is not the issue. If you think it is, go back to chapter one and Get Over Yourself. The question is… "What are you going to do about it today?"

God truly does want us to be in such a fellowship with Him on a daily basis that we can come to Him and confess our shortcomings. We all need to realize, however, that **Owning our Mess** is just the first step and in order to truly get out of whatever fish we are in, we will need to take action. Let's not make the mistake that so many people make in thinking that once an apology is uttered, all is well. Not quite. If you have **Owned your Mess** that is a wonderful thing but guess what: there's still a mess. This is the critical point where so many of us stop. There are still consequences or things that need to be done in order to fully clean up our mess. Usually, if we allow God to come back into our hearts at this point, He has a way of leading us through this process. It's not always pleasant, but it's always effective.

<u>Section III: "The GOOF Principle"</u>

Open UP

Psalm 139: 23-24

*Search me, O God, and know my heart; test me and know my
anxious thoughts. See if there is any offensive way in me, and
lead me in the way everlasting.*

(NIV)

Psalm 139: 23-24

*Investigate my life, O God, find out everything about me;
Cross-examine and test me, get a clear picture of what I'm
about; See for yourself whether I've done anything wrong—
then guide me on the road to eternal life.*

(The Message)

Take inventory: Where are you? Are you making progress in
getting out of your fish?

Get over yourself…

Own your mess….

Open up…..

F

Chapter 7

Hide & Seek

1 John 1: 9-10

If we confess our sins, he is faithful and just and will forgive us our sins and purify us from unrighteousness. If we claim we have not sinned we make him out to be a liar and his word has no place in our lives. (NIV)

1 John 1: 9-10

On the other hand, if we admit our sins—make a clean breast of them—he won't let us down; he'll be true to himself. He'll forgive our sins and purge us of all wrongdoing. If we claim that we've never sinned, we out-and-out contradict God—make a liar out of him. A claim like that only shows off our ignorance of God.

(The Message)

If we can get over ourselves and begin to own our part of the mess, then we need to keep pressing forward and experience the consequences of our actions so then there will be visible change. If you are truly prepared to get out of your fish and allow God to change your heart then owning the mess is one thing, but cleaning it up is another.

I think we often mistake confession with transformation. Confession is the key to transformation, but it doesn't automatically happen. We imagine that just owning up to our mistakes also fixes them, and this is why many of us never really allow God to completely transform our lives. It's almost like we play "Hide and Seek" with Him and our circumstances mostly in an effort to protect the all important ego and how others perceive us.

As a kid, "Hide and Seek" was one of those games that everyone loved to play. I would remember the feeling of excitement when you knew your hiding spot was awesome and no one could find you. You could hear people coming near sometimes, but they never found you. Some of us learned how to play this game into our adult lives, but with a twist. We have become masters at playing the game in plain sight of everyone around us. We play the adult version (young adults and children learn this too!) in broad daylight and justify or explain our faults in a way that make us feel better but don't affect any type of real change. We want all the accolades of being responsible and owning up to our mistakes, without the pain of actually taking the consequences.

Adam and Eve were the inventors of this game in the Garden of Eden. Their game of "Hide and Seek was mostly out of fear. They were fearful because of the sin they had committed, and the fact they knew something had dramatically changed in their relationship to the Creator.

They also quickly learned how to confess but not really take responsibility….

Genesis 3: 11b-13

… *"Have you eaten from the tree that I commanded you not to eat from?"*

The man said, "The woman you put here with me—she gave me some fruit and I ate it." Then the Lord God said to the woman, "What is this you have done?"

The woman said, "The serpent deceived me, and I ate."

Notice how they both admitted what they had done, but in doing so they avoided truly taking the blame. Adam immediately pointed to Eve, and Eve was already blaming the Devil.

Now, for all you guys out there who think it was Eve's fault because she forced Adam to eat the apple, let's have a reality check…

He took it.

He ate it.

Adam knew what he was doing, and so did Eve. They both wanted to have more knowledge and be like God. Eating from the tree of the knowledge of good and evil is what triggered the high stakes game of "Hide and Seek." Notice that before the picnic in the park, everything was fine. Adam and Eve had no shame and there was nothing to hide. Immediately after consuming the forbidden fruit, there was increased knowledge, (which they didn't know how to handle) awareness of their sin, and awareness of their nakedness. They both knew something had changed in their relationship to God, and it caused them to want to hide.

Genesis 3:8-10

Then the man and his wife heard the sound of the Lord God as he was walking in the garden in the cool of the day, and they hid from the Lord God among the trees of the garden. But the Lord God called to the man, "Where are you?"

He answered, "I heard you in the garden and I was afraid because I was naked; so I hid." (NIV)

If we are ever going to get to a place in our relationship to God where we fully trust Him, even when we mess up, then we must stop playing hide and seek. Jonah ran, hid, and tried everything possible to sleep through the storms of life. Finally however, he woke up, fessed up, and owned up. We must do the same.

Come to terms with the fact that we as human beings

can't handle the knowledge of good and evil. We have generationally let this knowledge paint us into corners of our own hearts that are riddled with judgment, bitterness, and self-righteousness. Perhaps that is why God didn't want us messing around that particular tree.

But if you are still hungry and want to chew on something, chew on this:

The knowledge of good and evil seems to be the aim of all ethical reflection. The first task of Christian ethics is to invalidate this knowledge.

Dietrich Bonhoeffer

If you don't know who Dietrich Bonhoeffer is….Google him. (you'll be blessed)

Jonah knew there was nowhere left to run and that God could not be deceived. This is the part where we must understand God's love for us and His desire that we just come clean and confess our mess with the full trust that He will forgive us. When Jonah finally owned up to the reality that it was his heart causing all the problems, that is when the groundwork was laid for God to use the fish to save him. Remember, the fish was what saved Jonah. The fish is where Jonah was humbled to the point of finding his first love again which was God himself. The fish is where Jonah realized he couldn't play hide and seek with God anymore and it was safe to come out, open his heart and give it all to God, fresh and new!

What kind of fish are you in?

Stop playing "Hide and Seek" and own your mess so God can begin the healing process. Trust me, He's not looking for you because He already knows where you are. The question is… **"Do you know where you are?"** Own your mess and let God all the way in so you can become a part of His purpose. Once you own it, you'll have to **Open Up** from within and allow God to find you. If you can do that, no matter how dire the circumstances, the game is over and you win.

Chapter 8

Is That Seaweed on Your Face?

Jonah 2: 1; 5

From inside the fish Jonah prayed to the Lord his God. He said:

(vs.5) The engulfing waters threatened me, the deep surrounded me; seaweed was wrapped around my head. (NIV)

Jonah was going down. He was literally sinking to the bottom of the ocean. The sailors threw him overboard, became Christians, and then probably had a party because the storm had subsided.   But Jonah was in deep.....literally.

When we become fully awake and wipe the sleep out of our eyes, it should dawn on us that we are in deep waters and we need God. If you are walking around right now suddenly realizing your life is going to wrong way or you are sinking fast into circumstances you don't want to be in then, oddly enough, you're in a good place. You probably have some seaweed wrapped around your head like Jonah, but don't worry, God has a way out for you.

The bitter, judgmental heart led to running and a serious storm for Jonah. It also affected the people he was with. Once he owned it, he was suffering the consequences and on his way to the bottom of the sea. God **PROVIDED** the fish and Jonah realized from within the belly of the fish, that God had saved him. More importantly, Jonah realized once again how Loving, Forgiving, and Merciful God is, and that there is only one thing in life that brings purpose; Serving Him.

Let's look at how this relates to all of us, in our culture today...

Example:

Our judgmental heart leads to envy and jealousy and coveting or wanting what we think others have.

We then pretend like everything is okay even though we harbor bad feelings about how we view ourselves and others. We start taking control of our own lives in a way that excludes God.

We start using credit and other means to obtain things we think we deserve. The storms are brewing. We get in over our head and end up sinking in debt with seaweed all over our face.

We finally wake up and God gives us a moment of clarity. We understand once again, that the Cross of Jesus Christ is all that matters and we have a desperate need of HIM. He shows us Grace.

We begin to Tithe, and get our finances back in order and God is in complete control of our lives.

Now, I know you're saying, "It's not that easy!" Yes, I agree. I didn't say it would be easy, I'm sure that's why God wrote: "Thou shall not covet", in that 10 commandments thing! We get ourselves into these messes and sometimes it's not easy getting out. The point is, we need to start understanding that God may not be punishing, He may be providing. He may just be saving our life with an unpleasant situation that is a result of our hard-heartedness. I'm betting the Fish was not a pleasant place for Jonah to be for three days and three nights, but it was the place where he opened his heart back up to God.

Open up

Psalm 32: 3-5

When I kept it all inside, my bones turned to powder, my words became daylong groans.

The pressure never let up; all the juices of my life dried up.

Then I let it all out; I said, "I'll make a clean breast of my failures to God."

Suddenly the pressure was gone—my guilt dissolved, my sin disappeared.

(The Message)

God does not want you to get to a place where you need Him to intervene in a dramatic way. He would prefer that your heart stay soft, and in tune with Him. I do not believe He causes us to get addicted, or get into debt or any other ill that is plaguing our world these days, but He will use our weakness to show His strength. However, if we find ourselves in a storm that lead to an unpleasant place like Jonah did, I beg you to start seeing clearly how God is providing a place for you to open up to Him. Wipe the seaweed from your eyes and quit trying to earn back His favor. You can't do it. He's in love with you right where you are. You cannot explain your way out of the fish, nor can you earn enough frequent flyer points with God to somehow get a free trip to Vomit Beach. God is patient, and He wants your heart. He has Grace for you. In fact, the fish you may be in is full of Grace if you'll have it.

Jonah 2: 8

"Those who cling to worthless idols forfeit the grace that could be theirs." (NIV)

Completely open up to God from wherever you're at and let Him clean house. The mistake we often make is that we subscribe to the old saying, "I got myself into this mess, and I'll get myself out." We do realize the need to get out, but we want to do it our way, in large part to maintain some sense of worth and protect our ego. God never operates that way. The harder we try to get out of the fish, the longer we will stay. I'll admit it is very hard to humble yourself and surrender all to God, thanking Him for who He is when all we can see is turmoil. But it is what Jonah did, and it's what we must do also. Opening up to God from within your difficult circumstance could just be exactly what He is waiting for. *BE ENCOURAGED!!*

Jonah 2: 1-2

From inside the fish Jonah prayed to the Lord his God. He said: "In my distress I called to the Lord, and he answered me.

From the depths of the grave I called for help, and you listened to my cry." (NIV)

Whatever circumstances you are going through right now, whatever struggles you have, if it stems from something in your heart, then you can bet God is focused on getting that part fixed first. Once He has your heart again, He will speak to your circumstance and it will change for the good. Nothing is going to change until you decide, from within your fish, to get totally reconnected to God in a way that allows Him to come fully into your heart.

You must come to terms with where you are at, and you must pray. But not your ordinary everyday type of prayer......something more like:

"Dear God, I totally, totally, totally, get it. I know I have made a mess of things because of my stubborn heart and my prideful actions. Thank you for letting me stew here, until I realized that EVERYTHING starts with YOU! EVERYTHING is about YOU! Thank you for not turning your back on me when I was judging people left and right and walking around with my nose in the air, because of my false sense of self-righteousness.....Thank you for saving me through your Grace, and the sacrifice Jesus made on the Cross. I need you. I do not like my circumstances, and I don't like the way it smells here in this fish. All I want is you. You have my heart again, so do whatever you have to do to keep it soft and in tune with YOU. Now, if it's not too much trouble, can you help me get this seaweed off my face and get me out of here?"

Don't be the Cornering kind

Opening up to God is the start of renewal, redemption, and the abundant life He wants for all of us. My advice to you is making sure you open up to God and not everyone around you! Start with God and let Him guide you through this process. I realize the need for relationships where you can share and open your heart to others for accountability (small groups) and to be encouraged, but too often those relationships take the place of God. If left unchecked, you become one of those people who want to share everything with everybody….ALL THE TIME!

You know how it goes….you're at a reunion or a church function and you run into someone and say, "How are you". Twenty five minutes later you are trying to get a word in to tell them you're late for a root canal, and that you hope their situation gets better.   I have found there are some people who are skilled enough to let weeks and sometimes months elapse in between sentences! (I think this naturally happens as we get older) You'll be minding your own business and walking down the aisle at the grocery store and all of the sudden you see the "Talker". You instantly remember your last conversation you had with them 6 months ago, (who can forget talking about foot fungus and unemployed cousin-in-laws!) and before you can get "hello" out of your mouth, it's game on. The "talker" doesn't even say hello, rather their shoe is coming off to show you the improvement regarding the foot issue. (You're having a hard time trying to remain conscious) The "talker" can multi-task too, because while all this is going on, they are also bringing you up to speed on the cousin-in-law, and opening up three new concerns they want to talk about, perhaps if not today, then the next time you see them at the gas station. We all have people like this in our life and sometimes I will tell you I have been the one doing the cornering. We do need to listen to those who are hurting, but we also need to be bold enough to encourage them to seek God's direction. Challenging them to honestly open up to what God is saying to them.

If you are in a fish, open up to God from within your heart and from within your circumstance and see what happens. Jonah opened up, by himself from within. It was one on one. We need to start there, and let God do the talking. We can praise Him, and thank Him, but we also need to listen. Let God lead as you open up your heart to Him and remember you are in His hands for a wonderful purpose.

Chapter 9

Opting Back into Life

Psalm 103: 1-5

Praise the Lord, O my soul; all my inmost being, praise his holy name. Praise the Lord, O my soul, and forget not all his benefits—who forgives all your sins and heals all your diseases. who redeems your life from the pit and crowns you with love and compassion, who satisfies your desires with good things so that your youth is renewed like the eagle's. (NIV)

Psalm 103: 1-5

O my soul, bless God. From head to toe, I'll bless his holy name!

O my soul, bless God, don't forget a single blessing!

He forgives your sins—every one.

He heals your diseases—every one.

He redeems you from hell—saves your life!

He crowns you with love and mercy—a paradise crown.

He wraps you in goodness—beauty eternal.

He renews your youth—you're always young in his presence.

(The Message)

Jonah was in a bad spot. He probably knew full well he had run from God, tried to sleep it off, and finally had to own up to the storm he caused. Now, he's inside the belly of a great fish. We don't know how or when Jonah realized that the fish was the provision of God, but we do know at some point Jonah began praising God from within the circumstance he was in. Jonah was deciding to not only open up to God, but also to opt back into life by praising God and proclaiming God's goodness. His prayers were not negotiations or manipulations. He was simply saying outloud all the things he knew about God and what God had done for him. It's amazing how quickly we all forget about the good things God does for us every day, even in the midst of bad situations.

It is a conscious decision for us to thank God in the middle of uncertain times. A decision to not want anything from Him, but choosing to praise Him for who He is. It unlocks the power of heaven and sets our hearts right at the same time.

Our prayer life, or the way we think about God when we are in a tough circumstance, will absolutely dictate how we navigate through it. If you think God owes you something because you tithe or attend church regularly, it's going to be a long and bumpy road. If you try and negotiate with God, and make deals based on how "good" you plan to be, then you are once again, missing the point. You can't make deals with God because the deal has already been made. He's God and you're not. That's the deal!

Jonah 2: 5-7

Ocean gripped me by the throat. The ancient Abyss grabbed me and head tight.

My head was all tangled in seaweed at the bottom of the sea where the mountains take root. I was as far down as a body can go, and the gates were slamming shut behind me forever— Yet you pulled from that grave alive, O God, my God!

When my life was slipping away, I remembered God, and my prayer got through to you, made it all the way to your Holy Temple. (The Message)

If you open your life up to God in a genuine way, He will not shame you, or make you feel guilty about your GOOFS. Let that sink in for awhile. Meditate on it. If you feel those emotions, they must be coming from somewhere else. Decide to get past it, and begin the process of **Opting Back In** to your life. The abundant life that God wants for you is there if you will let Him lead. Don't ever lose heart, and never give up. This is a critical stage in the process of opening up to God because our tendency is to feel good about it, and then continue to try things our way. Opt back in God's way, by staying close to Him, and following Him.

The longer we try to manipulate our own circumstances and hold on to our precious ego and pride, then the more creative God will be in getting your hearts attention. Jonah began to simply praise God and tell of His goodness. Jonah remembered how big, loving, and powerful the Lord is and how much grace and love he showed to Jonah. When Jonah realized his own hearts failures and how insignificant he was without God, he began to draw strength through admitting his weakness. Jonah began to experience God all over again through proclaiming who God is and admitting that all life starts, is sustained, and is in the hand of the Lord. From inside the fish, praising God is where Jonah drew close to God.

Jonah 2: 9-10

But I, with a song of thanksgiving, will sacrifice to you. What I have vowed I will make good. Salvation comes from the Lord.

And the Lord commanded the fish, and it vomited Jonah onto dry land. (NIV)

Did you catch that last part?

Once Jonah began to praise God and thank Him for who he is, things began to change. Jonah found strength through praising God and as a result, he vowed to sacrifice for God. Not begrudgingly and not because God was forcing him to. Jonah wanted to. He wanted to because he had once again discovered how awesome and loving and forgiving God truly is…..to everyone.

When Jonah's heart was right, God spoke to the fish and things changed for the good. When your heart is right, God will speak to your circumstance or your fish, or your mother-in-law…. "oops!" how did that get in there?

God will speak into your heart, then into your situation when He knows your heart has heard Him loud and clear. Wherever you're at in the process of getting out of your fish, just know that God loves you and has a purpose for your life. Don't give up and don't let the enemy or anyone else tell you that things can't change. It may seem like things will never change, and it would be so easy to give in and let your heart remain bitter or even become more hopeless and judgmental, but I'm begging you…..hold on, and press on.

Philippians 3: 13-14

Brothers, I do not consider myself yet to have taken hold of it. But one thing I do: Forgetting what is behind and straining toward what is ahead. I press on toward the goal to win the prize for which God has called me heavenward in Christ Jesus. (NIV)

> Be encouraged! You're almost out of your fish!!!! Make a decision to OPT BACK IN! Make a difference by letting God be God and with thanksgiving in your heart tell Him you vow to do whatever it takes to give Him your heart.

<u>Section IV: "The GOOF Principle"</u>

Forgive Yourself & Others

1 Timothy 1:15

Here is a trustworthy saying that deserves full acceptance: Christ Jesus came into the world to save sinners—of whom I am the worst. (NIV)

1 Timothy 1:15

Here's a word you can take to heart and depend on: Jesus Christ came into the world to save sinners. I'm proof—Public Sinner Number One.

This is one of the most, if not the most important aspects of fulfilling your destiny with God. Learning how to forget your mistakes, forgive yourself in a way so you're not living in the past, then forgiving others the same way that Christ forgave you.

Take inventory......be diligent, don't quit now.

Get over yourself

Own your mess

Open up to God

Forgive yourself & others

The GOOF principle is taking shape.......When you goof, (and you will) remember how to get yourself out!

Chapter 10

Seeing Clearly

Jonah 3: 1-2

Then the word of the Lord came to Jonah a second time: "Go to the great city of Nineveh and proclaim the message I give to you." (NIV)

God had commanded the fish to vomit Jonah onto dry land and there he stands dripping with an unknown substance, standing at attention perhaps saluting God saying, "Yes sir, right away sir!" I would probably be acting the same way because second chances always energize people for the moment and give us a renewed sense of purpose. Holding on to that energy and sense of purpose is what seems to elude us over time and as we will discover, it escaped Jonah as well.

Jonah was no doubt seeing very clearly and understood that God still wanted to use him for a big mission. It must have been good to know God had not given up on him even after running, napping, and causing hardcore sailors to soil their pants. Notice, there is no mention of Jonah trying to make up for his mistake. He simply obeyed. I have confessed many things in my life that I'm not proud of, mostly relating to pride, and what always seems to dampen my spirit soon afterwards is a sense that I must make up for disappointing God. The lesson here, is we need to know how to let go of our mistakes, and be free to experience God and His *Grace, Love, and Forgiveness.* We must learn to forgive ourselves and move on.

Now, we can't forgive ourselves of our own sin and earn our spot in heaven, but we can learn to defend ourselves against the lie that says we must sulk over our failures. There will always be a time to feel bad for our mistakes and it's healthy to feel this way for awhile, but we must decide to leave that behind and forgive ourselves and go forward. You cannot make things up to God by somehow feeling bad enough, or trying to be a martyr. It's like we want to write 200 sentences for God on some heavenly chalkboard that says, "I'm sorry I failed you......." It makes us feel better if we think we can somehow atone for our mistakes. Remember Section 1: Get Over Yourself! God doesn't need our self-serving humbleness and false promises, nor does He want to hold anything over our heads. He wants your heart. He loves you and wants you to be sold out to Him.

Trying to make up for things or keep everything on an even playing field never works in God's economy. The way we think of justice, doesn't always match up with the way God sees things. It just doesn't work out the way we think it should sometimes. As a result, we get frustrated and feel like our rights get trampled from time to time. The harder we try to make sense out of God's grace, the faster we will revert back to a heart condition that leads to swimming with the fishes.

There is an awesome parable in the Gospel of Matthew that talks about God's grace. The story found in chapter 20 illustrates how our definition of what's fair and just is totally different from God's definition. I'm no expert, but I would bet that God's definition is the only one that matters. The title of the story or parable is *The Parable of the Workers in the Vineyard* and I highly recommend you study it, and let it sink deep in to your soul. The basic premise is to reveal what the kingdom of Heaven is like through the story of a man who hired men at all hours of the day to come and work in his vineyard. At the end of the day when it was time to pay the men, those who worked the least amount of time got paid first. They received a full days wage for only working an hour! (That's whacked out!) Well, obviously the men who were hired early in the morning were thinking that they would get way more than the bums who only put in an hour. It was bad enough that they had worked the longest and had to wait and be the last ones paid, but they probably figured it will be worth it because they would be getting some overtime pay. It didn't go down like that. The men who worked all day got the exact same pay as those who only worked an hour. They obviously grumbled and they had every right, right? Well, not according to God because His GRACE is the great equalizer. This is the point of the parable and even though the example used was money and time, the point is that the kingdom of heaven is not anything like how things operate in our culture. Here are the key verses:

Matthew 20: 15-16

"Don't I have the right to do what I want with my own money? Or are you envious because I am generous? So the last will be first, and the first will be last." (NIV)

We need to just accept that we don't know everything about how or why God does what he does. We should just be thankful that He has grace for all of us. Forgive yourself for being a bonehead and don't walk around thinking God owes you anything special for a string of good behavior. This is the key to staying out of future fish. Do whatever you have to do to keep you heart soft and your vision clear. Just remember God's ways are not our ways. Thank goodness!

Jonah got right back to work once God delivered him from the fish and didn't waste time moping around. He went to Nineveh, which would be like me going to Las Vegas and standing on the Strip warning the people of their actions against God. (Of course, I wouldn't mind giving someone a buck or two to lay on black, just in case God was smiling on me!) Now, in my heart I'm thinking that these jokers don't deserve any chance to turn their lives around because it's obvious they want nothing to do with God. This is the trap we fall into, and it starts to harden our hearts all over again. Jonah fell into the same trap.

Hanging On To Stupid

Jonah completed the mission and sat back and watched for what would happen. God did not destroy Nineveh, and as a result of Jonah's preaching, the whole place got on their knees and repented. Starting with the King and on down the line everyone prayed, fasted, and dedicated themselves to God. It's a good thing .....right? Don't ask Jonah. He went right back to a self-centered way of thinking and got bent because God spared them. Jonah did *his* job but then somehow still thought that they all deserved the wrath of God.

Jonah 4: 1-3

But Jonah was greatly displeased and became angry. He prayed to the Lord, "O Lord, is this not what I said when I was still at home? That is why I was so quick to flee to Tarshish. I knew that you are a gracious and compassionate God slow to anger and abounding in love, a God who relents from sending calamity. Now, O Lord, take away my life, for it is better for me to die than to live." (NIV)

How many times in our life do we soften up to the point that we extend grace to someone but it has limitations or conditions? We want to feel like we've done our part but deep down we think they should experience the consequences of their actions because it settles some cosmic scorecard we all carry around in our pocket. We store up these informational scorecards in our heart, and we secretly hang onto them in the most perverse way. If we are not careful, our hearts can snap back to judgment, envy, and disdain quicker than my own 14 year old son can text message.

If we are going to continually revert back into our old way of thinking and behaving, then forgiving our GOOFS doesn't mean a thing. God wants us in a constant state of awareness to the way we should extend grace, forgive others, and go the extra mile. The moment we begin to hold on to junk in our hearts is the moment we dare God to send another fish in our direction. As our hearts fill up with junk, it's very difficult to see clearly.

Matthew 7: 1-5

"Don't pick on people, jump on their failures, criticize their faults—unless of course, you want the same treatment. That critical spirit has a way of boomeranging. It's easy to see a smudge on your neighbor's face and be oblivious to the ugly sneer on your own. Do you have the nerve to say, 'Let me wash your face for you,' when your own face is distorted by contempt? It's the whole traveling road-show mentality all over again, playing a holier-than-thou part instead of just living your part. Wipe that ugly sneer off your own face, and you might be fit to offer a washcloth to your neighbor."

(The Message)

> Forgive yourself for being a bonehead and don't walk around thinking God owes you anything special for a string of good behavior.

Chapter 11

Teaching Moments

God is Sovereign

Jonah 4: 6-9a

Then the Lord God provided a vine and made it grow up over Jonah to give shade for his head to ease his discomfort, and Jonah was very happy about the vine. But at dawn the next day God provided a worm, which chewed the vine so that it withered. When the sun rose, God provided a scorching east wind, and the sun blazed on Jonah's head so that he grew faint. He wanted to die, and said, "It would be better for me to die than to live."

But God said to Jonah, "Do you have a right to be angry about the vine?" (NIV)

Rights, Rights, Rights!!! We live in a culture that has made it all about rights, and that we should seek, take by force, or scream at the top of our lungs until we get our rights.

There is a HUGE difference between being Politically Correct, and Biblically Correct. Trying to live in a politically correct world so that our rights and everyone else's are protected is absurd because there's no end to the pursuit. No one is ever satisfied, and someone is always upset. Life always is experienced more abundantly when we understand:

1. God is Sovereign

2. It's not our rights that He is concerned about

3. His Kingdom takes priority over EVERYTHING!

God was definitely providing Jonah with some teaching moments as we can see from the scripture above. The two fold message was that God is sovereign and Jonah was sliding back in to a state of selfishness. God provided the vine to ease Jonah's discomfort and when it was taken away, Jonah became angry. God was not playing games with Jonah, He was revealing that Jonah should be less worried about the things he can't control and more worried about the things that really matter.

The vine represents our attachment to what we think we deserve. This mentality in our culture needs to be shaken to its core because it is destructive and keeps us in a state of confusion. There were a huge number of people in Nineveh that God wanted to reach, and Jonah was angry about the vine. When we think of it that way, it seems obvious that Jonah was being pretty selfish, and that God did a good job in that particular teaching moment. My question for you is… "What *vine* are you hanging on to and becoming angry about because it's not working out the way you think it should?" Is it your rights?

Philippians 2: 3-8

Do nothing out of selfish ambition or vain conceit, but in humility consider others better than yourselves. Each of you should look not only to your own interests, but also to the interests of others.

Your attitude should be the same as that of Christ Jesus: Who being in very nature God, did not consider equality with God something to be grasped, but made himself nothing, taking the very nature of a servant, being made in human likeness.

And being found in appearance as a man, he humbled himself and became obedient to death—even death on a cross!

God loves you dearly, and He is ultimately in control of all things. You can either be a slave to what you think is your right, or you can surrender to Him, taking comfort in knowing He's got it covered. Take a deep breath and realize that you don't have to work so hard to maintain your significance. Stop living in fear of not having a voice. Let Him be your voice, and let Him be your shelter. Let Him be everything, and you will *find* your voice.

Psalm 56: 3-4

When I am afraid, I will trust in you. In God, whose word I praise, in God I trust; I will not be afraid. What can mortal man do to me? (NIV)

God's sovereignty is something that is often misunderstood and our lack of understanding it is what creates the confusion between what we think we deserve, and how the world should work. If you are going to stay clear of future fish in your life, just try and see the world as God does and let your heart be used of Him to serve a greater purpose.

Today more than ever, Christians and non-Christians are starting to resemble one another to the point it is hard to tell them apart. The salt is losing it's saltiness, and the light is hard to find sometimes. Christians are becoming lukewarm at best and "Church Life" has started to look and feel more like a Country Club than a place for Worship. Nice buildings are not the problem, it's the people inside who are constantly running, napping, and hiding from God.

"To those in the West, the bigger the number of respondents, the more replicated the technique. The bigger the statistic, the greater the success. Westerners are enamored by size, largesse, number of

hands raised, and so on. When the sun has set on these reports, we seem rather dismayed when statistics show the quality of the life of the believer is no different from that of the unbeliever." (Ravi Zacharias; Beyond Opinion)

Ouch! What does this mean?? It means there is a Jonah quality in all of us that needs to wake up, own up, and be sold out for God, no matter what it looks like to everyone else.

You would think that after you become a Christian and allow your heart to be totally surrendered to God that things would get easier. Not always true. Overall, there is a peace and a joy that come from knowing Jesus Christ as your Lord but life still happens and God is always operating with a bigger picture in mind.

John 16: 33

"I have told you these things, so that in me you may have peace. In this world you will have trouble. But take heart I have overcome the world." (NIV)

Chicken Pox & a Sobering Revelation... Why Not Me?

I had been a Christian for about 3 years and was still enamored with my new relationship with God. I felt fully alive for the first time in a long time and I loved spending time with Jesus reading the Bible and praying. My church was and still is very important to me and my family and I love them all dearly. You need to try and grasp what I am about to share with you because there are so many people out there that still equate religion and being a Christian as having no problems and being perfect. Not the case.

I would argue that the real war never even gets going until you declare your heart has been given over to God. Then all Hell breaks loose. I was 36 years old and trying desperately to unwind a financial crisis that my family and I were going through due to a company relocation that decided not to relocate me along with them! I was coaching a youth basketball team at the time and as if the stress of the financial burden wasn't enough, one of the 7 year olds I was coaching comes in with Chicken Pox. My mom informed me that I had never had the Chicken Pox as a kid and back then there was no vaccine. The little "booger" who gave me the Chicken Pox was back playing ball the next week. ..I however, was in for the ride of my life.

I had heard that Adult Chicken Pox could be serious so I called my friend Dr. Mike. Now, Dr. Mike is a guy who is never rattled by anything, and I was sure he was going to tell me not to worry. Dr. Mike is notorious for saying things like "shake it off", or "You'll be alright, quit your whining". If I were to call him and say that my arm was broken and swollen to the size of a watermelon, his response would be…. "Use your other arm!"

All kidding aside, Mike is a great Dr. and a great friend so I called him because I was a little scared. I got him on the phone and told him what was going on. His tone was much different than normal and there was a lack of jovialness to the conversation. Dr. Mike told me it could be serious and in some cases things can get out of hand.

My spiritual life as a Christian was still considered to be pretty young and immature. I was learning and growing in my faith. I loved God but I also knew I was harboring some judgmental and arrogant attitudes in my heart. I do not believe God caused me to get sick, but I have since learned that I'm sure He used it to bring me to a point of awareness and surrender so I could go deeper in my relationship and begin to understand a little bit more about His sovereignty and His grace.

My first trip to the Emergency Room came at the end of week one with the Chicken Pox. My internal organs were being affected and I was having severe stomach pain. Upon arriving at the E.R. some time close to midnight, I noticed there wasn't much activity. The doctors and nurses probably thought they were in for another long boring night. I walked in, and everything changed! I noticed all their faces lighting up and I even sensed some weird kind of excitement as if they had just hit the "E. R. Lottery" or something. They needed to keep me in quarantine so they stuck me in an old examination room that was rarely used. (I think it's where doctors would doze off in the middle of the night) I honestly felt like I was the main attraction at a Carnival Freak Show. I was expecting someone to start barking out, "Step right up and see the Human Chicken Man! He's part human, part chicken pox, a real sight to see!"

One of the nurses had gotten really excited because they were training a young nursing school student that night. I faintly remember someone saying, "This is awesome, we'll be able to show our young nursing student a real live case of adult chicken pox, how lucky is that?" Well, they brought the young nursing student into the room so she could observe. She lasted about 7 seconds. I knew for sure she was questioning the career decision she had made. I've got $20 bucks right now that says that young girl dropped out of nursing school the next day.

Well, I got some pain medication and went back home, but they did run some tests and told me to watch for stiffness in my neck. If I felt any stiffness at all I needed to get back to the hospital ASAP. They warned me sometimes adult chicken pox can lead to meningitis. If it was viral, it could be really bad. So guess what? About 4 days later I woke up at 5:15 a.m. with a stiff neck. I felt awful and it seemed things were just going to continue to get worse.

I remember telling my wife to stay in bed but that I was heading back to the E. R. because my neck was really stiff. I was well enough to drive myself, but mentally I was struggling. I kept telling myself this is bad and if I have waited too long or they can't help me then this could be very bad. It was the first time in my life that I actually thought I could die. My recurring thought was, "not like this....not chicken pox, then meningitis...not this way Lord." Then it turned into, "Why me? Why now? What's the purpose?" Mostly, however, it was, "Why me?"

Then in an instant, I encountered a strange and peaceful silence. I heard God in my spirit gently say, "Why not you Jay?" I stopped talking out loud at this point and I was in full silence mode. A peace was surrounding me and as I reflected for a moment and started to let go of all the worry and all the junk in my heart, strangely enough the response made sense. God is in complete control and I realized it maybe for the first time in my life. I was seeing things from a different view. I didn't want to die, but I just knew I was safe because God was in complete control of the situation. He is sovereign and He is the meaning of everything.

Let me ask a question. If God would have called me to heaven that morning, in that way because He knew that 10 of my friends and family who don't know Jesus would have come to know Him through my story and my circumstances would that have been okay? I would have to answer yes.

Well, since I'm sitting here writing this book, I guess you've figured out that God spared me and has something left for me to do. I've got some scars on my face from the Chicken Pox, and my pride still rears its ugly head from time to time, but down deep in my soul, Jesus has left His mark on me. I'm so glad He did. Through all the ups and downs of life, and the pain that comes from suffering, doubt, and failures I can truly say my faith in the Cross and Jesus Christ has not wavered. He is always there with me, and He will not leave me. He is my Lord, and I'm learning how to love Him more and more each day.

If I truly consider myself to be a follower of Jesus Christ, the statement I hang my hat on is "Why not me." When things get tough or things don't start to make sense I try to take a step back and remember that God is in complete control and I will never know everything He is up to until I get to Heaven. It's not always easy in our culture that teaches a *"me first"* mentality.

I must confess to you that I still struggle with what I'm trying to encourage you to do in this last section: Forgive yourself & Others. After God delivered me from my addiction to alcohol I went through a period of my life, just like Jonah, where I was very happy to have been set free, but I was quick to judge. I would be quick to point fingers at those who in my mind were not living right. When it came to forgiving myself for my years of causing others pain, well, that was nowhere on my radar screen. Make no mistake, I had given my life to Jesus Christ, and I knew I was free from sin and the stronghold of alcohol and I couldn't have been happier. The reality, however, was I was just an infant in my faith. Like all infants I was needy, loud, and could wreck a dinner party! As I look back, I'm so thankful that God's grace and forgiveness continues in my life because I need it everyday. As time has gone on I have grown in God's grace and my understanding of His Love for all people. I reach out often with Love and hope to make a difference in people's live who are hurting with the story of Christ. But now, I realize the one person I still have trouble forgiving is myself. Jesus died for my sins, but for some reason I'm still trying to make up for them. I have caused a lot of pain to myself and others and I struggle with forgiving myself for my mistakes. In a weird way it's another form of pride that I think I'll be dealing with for the rest of my life. I pray not.

We are called to lose our life so we can find it. God is full of mercy and grace for all people and He wants all to know him. As long as we think we are above any suffering or that we are someone special, then we will struggle to understand God's character. Make no mistake, YOU ARE SPECIAL......but only because God loves you and has a purpose for your life that is bigger than you think.

You can do nothing to become more special to Him than you are right now. So relax and enjoy the peace from knowing He is in complete control. I truly hope you will apply the principles in this book to help you maintain a vibrant, growing relationship with God. He wants you to live an abundant life with Him, so it's time to Get Out Of the Fish!

Get Over Yourself

Own Your Mess

Open Up to God

Forgive Yourself and Others

If you do not know where you stand with God, please contact a local church that teaches Jesus Christ as Lord and the Cross as the only way to God. Or, pray this prayer right where you are. If you do, go to my website jayharveyministries.com and let me know. God bless you!

Lord, I know I have fallen short, and that I need forgiveness. I am repenting of my ways, and now turning to Jesus Christ for forgiveness. I accept Jesus all the way into my heart and want to live for Him. I believe He is the Son of God, and was resurrected, and that the Cross is where my sins were forgiven.

Come into my life, and be my Lord and Savior. In Jesus name, amen.